Farewell to Model T

❖

From Sea to Shining Sea

Farewell to Model T

E. B. WHITE

From Sea to Shining Sea

THE LITTLE BOOKROOM
New York

© E. B. White

Designed by Katy Homans, New York

Cover photo: Katharine and E. B. White in a 1923 Model T Ford (not Hotspur),
Brooklin, Maine, c. 1940. Other photographs accompanying the text were taken
during E. B. White's cross country trip in 1922.
All photographs courtesy of Allene White.

Library of Congress Cataloging-in-Publication Data

White, E. B. (Elwyn Brooks), 1899–
Farewell to Model T ; From sea to shining sea / E.B. White.
p. cm.
ISBN 1-892145-21-9
1. White, E. B. (Elwyn Brooks), 1899—Journeys—United States. 2.
Automobile travel—United States. 3. Ford Model T automobile. I.
Title: Farewell to Model T ; From sea to shining sea. II. White, E. B.
(Elwyn Brooks), 1899– From sea to shining sea. III. Strout, Richard L.
(Richard Lee), 1898– IV. Title: From sea to shining sea. V. Title.
PS3545.H5187 F37 2003
818'.52—dc21

2002152148

Second Printing September 2003
10 9 8 7 6 5 4 3 2

The Little Bookroom
1755 Broadway, 5th floor
New York NY 10019
T (212) 293-1643
F (212) 333-5374
editorial@littlebookroom.com
www.littlebookroom.com

to Henry Ford

Farewell to Model T
1936

Farewell to Model T

I see by the new Sears Roebuck catalogue that it is still possible to buy an axle for a 1909 Model T Ford, but I am not deceived. The great days have faded, the end is in sight. Only one page in the current catalogue is devoted to parts and accessories for the Model T; yet everyone remembers springtimes when the Ford gadget section was larger than men's clothing, almost as large as household furnishings. The last Model T was built in 1927, and the car is fading from what scholars call the American scene—which is an understatement, because to a few million people who grew up with it, the old Ford practically *was* the American scene.

It was the miracle God had wrought. And it was patently the sort of thing that could only happen once. Mechanically uncanny, it was like nothing that had ever come to the world before. Flourishing industries rose and fell with it. As a vehicle, it was hard-working, commonplace, heroic; and it often seemed to transmit those qualities to the persons who rode in it. My own generation identifies it with Youth, with its gaudy, irretrievable excitements; before it fades into the mist, I would like to pay it the tribute of the sigh that is not a sob, and set down random entries in a shape somewhat less cumbersome than a Sears Roebuck catalogue.

The Model T was distinguished from all other makes of cars by the fact that its transmission was of a type known as planetary—which was half metaphysics, half sheer friction. Engineers accepted the word "planetary" in its epicyclic sense, but I was always conscious that it also meant "wandering," "erratic." Because of the peculiar nature of this planetary element, there was always, in Model T, a certain dull rapport between engine and wheels, and even when the car was in a state known as neutral, it trembled with a deep imperative and tended to inch forward. There was never a moment when the bands were not faintly egging the machine on. In this respect it was like a horse, rolling the bit on its tongue, and country people brought to it the same technique they used with draft animals.

Its most remarkable quality was its rate of acceleration. In its palmy days the Model T could take off faster than anything on the road. The reason was simple. To get under way, you simply hooked the third finger of the right hand around a lever on the steering column, pulled down hard, and shoved your left foot forcibly against the low-speed pedal. These were simple, positive motions; the car responded by lunging forward with a roar. After a few seconds of this turmoil, you took your toe off the pedal, eased up a mite on the throttle, and the car, possessed of only two forward speeds, catapulted directly into high with a series of ugly jerks and was off on its glorious errand. The abruptness of this departure was never equalled in other cars of the period. The human leg was (and still is) incapable of letting in a clutch with anything like the forthright abandon that used to send Model T on its way. Letting in a clutch is a negative, hesitant motion, depending on delicate nervous control; pushing down the Ford pedal was a simple, country motion—an expansive act, which came as natural as kicking an old door to make it budge.

The driver of the old Model T was a man enthroned. The car, with top up, stood seven feet high. The driver sat on top of the gas tank, brooding it with his own body. When he wanted gasoline, he alighted, along with everything else in the front seat; the seat was pulled off, the metal cap unscrewed, and a wooden stick thrust down to sound the liquid in the well. There were always a couple of these sounding sticks kicking around in the ratty sub-cushion regions of a flivver. Refuelling was more of a social function then, because the driver had to unbend, whether he wanted to or not. Directly in front of the driver was the windshield— high, uncompromisingly erect. Nobody talked about air resistance, and the four cylinders pushed the car through the atmosphere with a simple disregard of physical law.

There was this about a Model T: the purchaser never regarded his purchase as a complete, finished product. When you bought a Ford, you figured you had a start—a vibrant, spirited framework to which could be screwed an almost limitless assortment of decorative and functional hardware. Driving away from the agency, hugging the new wheel between your knees, you were already full of creative worry. A Ford was born naked as a baby, and a flourishing industry grew up out of correcting its rare deficiencies and combatting its fascinating diseases. Those were the great days of lily-painting. I have been looking at some old Sears Roebuck catalogues, and they bring everything back so clear.

First you bought a Ruby Safety Reflector for the rear, so that your posterior would glow in another car's brilliance. Then you invested thirty-nine cents in some radiator Moto Wings, a popular ornament which gave the Pegasus touch to the machine and did something god-like to the owner. For nine cents you bought a fan-belt guide to keep the belt from slipping off the pulley.

You bought a radiator compound to stop leaks.

This was as much a part of everybody's equipment as aspirin tablets are of a medicine cabinet. You bought special oil to prevent chattering, a clamp-on dash light, a patching outfit, a tool box which you bolted to the running board, a sun visor, a steering-column brace to keep the column rigid, and a set of emergency containers for gas, oil, and water—three thin, disc-like cans which reposed in a case on the running board during long, important journeys—red for gas, gray for water, green for oil. It was only a beginning. After the car was about a year old, steps were taken to check the alarming disintegration. (Model T was full of tumors, but they were benign.) A set of anti-rattlers (98c) was a popular panacea. You hooked them on to the gas and spark rods, to the brake pull rod, and to the steering-rod connections. Hood silencers, of black rubber, were applied to the fluttering hood. Shock-absorbers and snubbers gave "complete relaxation." Some people bought rubber pedal pads, to fit over the standard metal pedals. (I didn't like these, I remember.) Persons of a suspicious or pugnacious turn of mind bought a rear-view mirror; but most Model T owners weren't worried by what was coming from behind because they would soon enough see it out in front. They rode in a state of cheerful catalepsy. Quite a large mutinous clique among Ford owners went over to a foot accelerator (you could buy one and screw it to the floor board), but there was a certain madness in these people, because the Model T, just as she stood, had a choice of three foot pedals to push, and there were plenty of moments when both feet were occupied in the routine performance of duty and when the only way to speed up the engine was with the hand throttle.

Gadget bred gadget. Owners not only bought ready-made gadgets, they invented gadgets to meet special needs. I myself drove my car directly from the agency to the blacksmith's, and had the smith affix two enormous iron brackets to the port running board to support an army trunk.

People who owned closed models builded along different lines: they bought ball grip handles for opening doors, window anti-rattlers, and de-luxe flower vases of the cut-glass anti-splash type. People with delicate sensibilities garnished their car with a device called the Donna Lee Automobile Disseminator—a porous vase guaranteed, according to Sears, to fill the car with a "faint clean odor of lavender."

The gap between open cars and closed cars was not as great then as it is now: for $11.95, Sears Roebuck converted your touring car into a sedan and you went forth renewed. One agreeable quality of the old Fords was that they had no bumpers, and their fenders softened and wilted with the years and permitted the driver to squeeze in and out of tight places.

Tires were 30 x $3\frac{1}{2}$, cost about twelve dollars, and punctured readily. Everybody carried a Jiffy patching set, with a nutmeg grater to roughen the tube before the goo was spread on. Everybody was capable of putting on a patch, expected to have to, and did have to.

During my association with Model T's, self-starters were not a prevalent accessory. They were expensive and under suspicion. Your car came equipped with a serviceable crank, and the first thing you learned was how to Get Results. It was a special trick, and until you learned it (usually from another Ford owner, but sometimes by a period of appalling experimentation) you might as well have been winding up an awning. The trick was to leave the ignition switch off, proceed to the animal's head, pull the choke (which was a little wire protruding through the radiator), and give the crank two or three nonchalant upward lifts. Then, whistling as though thinking about something else, you would saunter back to the driver's cabin, turn the ignition on, return to the crank, and this time, catching it on the down stroke, give it a quick spin with plenty of That. If this procedure was followed, the engine almost always responded—first with a few scattered explosions, then with a tumultuous gunfire, which you checked by racing around to the driver's seat and retarding the throttle. Often, if the emergency brake hadn't been pulled all the way back, the car advanced on you the instant the first explosion occurred and you would hold it back by leaning your weight against it. I can still feel my old Ford nuzzling me at the curb, as though looking for an apple in my pocket.

In zero weather, ordinary cranking became an impossibility, except for giants. The oil thickened, and it became necessary to jack up the rear wheels, which, for some planetary reason, eased the throw.

The lore and legend that governed the Ford were boundless. Owners had their own theories about everything; they discussed mutual problems in that wise, infinitely resourceful way old women discuss rheumatism. Exact knowledge was pretty scarce, and often proved less effective than superstition. Dropping a camphor ball into the gas tank was a popular expedient; it seemed to have a tonic effect on both man and machine. There wasn't much to base exact knowledge on. The Ford driver flew blind. He didn't know the temperature of his engine, the speed of his car, the amount of his fuel, or the pressure of his oil (the old Ford lubricated itself by what was amiably described as the "splash system"). A speedometer cost money and was an extra, like a windshield-wiper. The dashboard of the early models was bare save for an ignition key; later models, grown effete, boasted an ammeter which pulsated alarmingly with the throbbing of the car. Under the dash was a box of coils, with vibrators which you adjusted, or thought you adjusted.

Whatever the driver learned of his motor, he learned not through instruments but through sudden developments. I remember that the timer was one of the vital organs about which there was ample doctrine. When everything else had been checked, you "had a look" at the timer. It was an extravagantly odd little device, simple in construction, mysterious in function. It contained a roller, held by a spring, and there were four contact points on the inside of the case against which, many people believed, the roller rolled. I have had a timer apart on a sick Ford many times, but I never really knew what I was up to—I was just showing off before God.

There were almost as many schools of thought as there were timers. Some people, when things went wrong, just clenched their teeth and gave the timer a smart crack with a wrench. Other people opened it up and blew on it. There was a school that held that the timer needed large amounts of oil; they fixed it by frequent baptism. And there was a school that was positive it was meant to run dry as a bone; these people were continually taking it off and wiping it.

I remember once spitting into a timer; not in anger, but in a spirit of research. You see, the Model T driver moved in the realm of metaphysics. He believed his car could be hexed.

One reason the Ford anatomy was never reduced to an exact science was that, having "fixed" it, the owner couldn't honestly claim that the treatment had brought about the cure. There were too many authenticated cases of Fords fixing themselves—restored naturally to health after a short rest. Farmers soon discovered this, and it fitted nicely with their draft-horse philosophy: "Let 'er cool off and she'll snap into it again."

A Ford owner had Number One Bearing constantly in mind. This bearing, being at the front end of the motor, was the one that always burned out, because the oil didn't reach it when the car was climbing hills. (That's what I was always told, anyway.) The oil used to recede and leave Number One dry as a clam flat; you had to watch that bearing like a hawk. It was like a weak heart—you could hear it start knocking, and that was when you stopped and let her cool off. Try as you would to keep the oil supply right, in the end Number One always went out. "Number One Bearing burned out on me and I had to have her replaced," you would say, wisely; and your companions always had a lot to tell about how to protect and pamper Number One to keep her alive.

Sprinkled not too liberally among the millions of amateur witch doctors who drove Fords and applied their own abominable cures were the heaven-sent mechanics who could really make the car talk. These professionals turned up in undreamed-of spots. One time, on the banks of the Columbia River in Washington, I heard the rear end go out of my Model T when I was trying to whip it up a steep incline onto the deck of a ferry. Something snapped; the car slid backward into the mud. It seemed to me like the end of the trail. But the captain of the ferry, observing the withered remnant, spoke up.

"What's got her?" he asked.

"I guess it's the rear end," I replied, listlessly. The captain leaned over the rail and stared. Then I saw that there was a hunger in his eyes that set him off from other men.

"Tell you what," he said, carelessly, trying to cover

up his eagerness, "let's pull the son of a bitch up onto the boat, and I'll help you fix her while we're going back and forth on the river."

We did just this. All that day I plied between the towns of Pasco and Kennewick, while the skipper (who had once worked in a Ford garage) directed the amazing work of resetting the bones of my car.

Springtime in the heyday of the Model T was a delirious season. Owning a car was still a major excitement, roads were still wonderful and bad. The Fords were obviously conceived in madness: any car which was capable of going from forward into reverse without any perceptible mechanical hiatus was bound to be a mighty challenging thing to the human imagination. Boys used to veer them off the highway into a level pasture and run wild with them, as though they were cutting up with a girl.

Most everybody used the reverse pedal quite as much as the regular foot brake—it distributed the wear over the bands and wore them all down evenly. That was the big trick, to wear all the bands down evenly, so that the final chattering would be total and the whole unit scream for renewal.

The days were golden, the nights were dim and strange. I still recall with trembling those loud, nocturnal crises when you drew up to a signpost and raced the engine so the lights would be bright enough to read destinations by. I have never been really planetary since. I suppose it's time to say good-bye. Farewell, my lovely!

From Sea to Shining Sea

1953

From Sea to Shining Sea

I located America thirty-one years ago in a Model T Ford and planted my flag. I've tried a couple of times since to find it again, riding in faster cars and on better roads, but America is the sort of place that is discovered only once by any one man.

When I set out with another fellow in 1922, it was spring, and I was young, and my little black roadster was young and new and blithe and gay. Everything lay ahead, and we had plenty of time of day: the land stretched interminably into the west and into the imaginations of young men. Our car seemed full of a deep inner excitement, just as we did ourselves. The highway was a blazed trail of paint-rings on telegraph poles, a westering trace marked by arrows whittled out of shingles and tacked negligently to the handiest tree. In many places the highway seemed non-existent—just a couple of ruts in the plain—but the Model T was not a fussy car. It sprang cheerfully toward any stretch of wasteland whether there was a noticeable road under foot or not. It had clearance, it had guts, and it enjoyed wonderful health.

My friend and I left New York on a raw March day and brought Poughkeepsie abeam by nightfall. Six months later we pulled into Seattle, leaving a track across the United States as erratic as a mouse's track in snow. The T is still to me a symbol of delicious delay. Structurally it was carefree, for it didn't give a hoot whether it was in high, low, neutral, reverse or any combination of the four, and would leap joyously from one to another with unbelievable abandon and success.

In two respects it was an exceptionally safe car: first, it didn't go very fast; second, it had three foot pedals and no matter which one of the three you pushed, your speed would be reduced. The really skillful driver, wishing to reduce speed, would apply first the brake, then a dab of low, then slide out of low into neutral (which meant letting the lefthand pedal relax into that twilight zone between high and low, a position so vague, so intermediate, that it was like a position on a violin string between two notes), then another dab of the brake, or, if he felt whimsical, a dash of reverse—unorthodox, perhaps, but perfectly acceptable to the wild planetary bands below the floorboards. Like a horse answering the reins, the T would answer its bands, responding brilliantly to the driver's excesses and uttering good-natured groans of mechanical compliance.

As a gesture of contempt—or perhaps as an earnest of high resolve—my companion and I left our Automobile Blue Book behind when we started west in 1922. We took along instead a Webster's Unabridged Dictionary, to serve as a constant reminder that our true destination was the world of letters.

I suppose modern youngsters have never laid eyes on a Blue Book, that Bible of touring in the early years of the century. The passenger on the seat with the driver held the Book open in his lap; he kept an eye on the mileage indicator on the dash, he kept an eye on landmarks, and he checked both with the printed story as it unfolded. Every tenth mile had to be corroborated by the surroundings. At 11.8 there must be a saloon on the left; "turn left, picking up trolley." (One was forever picking up trolleys in those days, and some of them were heavy indeed.) "11.9 Turn right with trolley on Burley Ave. Cross R.R. 12.3, jogging left and right . . ." The information was passed along to the driver, who, eyes front, jogged left and right, full of accomplishment, happy as a grig. Here were directions infinitely painstaking and exact. Forty times a day they saved you from some gaudy fate. The Blue Book not only described and unfolded the road, but the very process of comparison—the printed page with the visible landscape—was an absorbing adventure in itself and had the same hypnotic effect as working out a double crostic. A watering trough, looming at the predicted moment, was as welcome a sight to the motorist as is a spar-buoy to a mariner picking his way in the fog.

The Blue Book was a mine of curious and critical information. It pulled no punches. A road was "vile." A house (where you must turn sharp right) was "unpainted." A righthand fork (not recommended) was a "by-road into swamp." The Philadelphia-Pittsburgh turnpike was "a reproach to the State of

Pennsylvania." An important product of Elgin, Illinois was "coffin trimmings." Twenty-five miles an hour was "presumptive evidence of carelessness"—and one's mind went back to those trimmings.

A characteristic entry in the Blue Book went something like this: "38.8 Cross iron bridge, and at forks beyond, bear right, coming into Main Street." The words are beautiful in my heart. How many times have I crossed that bridge, borne right at the fork and come into Main Street! I can shut my eyes now and come into Main Street at the wheel of Model T, can experience again the sense of errantry, the sense of discovery, the excitement of arrival in a strange town. My left leg is languidly draped over the side, to indicate an easy familiarity with my mount. The hand throttle is at second notch, easing her along at a trickle. A whisper of dust curls in the wake. There are no cars ahead, no cars behind; we are the new arrivals—we have the stage to ourselves. Bystanders give us the eye. Main Street sprawls contented in the sun, and every third vehicle drowsing at the curb is a blood relation of the T.

To an American, the physical fact of the complete America is, at best, a dream, a belief, a memory, and the sound of names. My own vision of the land—my own discovery of its size and meaning—was shaped, more than by any other instrument, by a Model T Ford. The vision endures; the small black roadster is always there, alive and kicking, a bedroll wedged against its spare, a dictionary sprawling on its floor, an Army trunk bracketed to its left running board. The course of my life was changed by it, and it is in a class by itself. It was cheap enough so I could afford to buy one; it was capable enough so it gave me courage to start.

Youth, I have no doubt, will always recognize its own frontier and push beyond it by whatever means are at hand. As for me, I've always been glad that mine was a two-track road running across the prairie into the sinking sun, and underneath me a slow-motion roadster of miraculous design—strong, tremulous, and tireless, from sea to shining sea.